Hocus Pocus

The Magical Power of St. Peter

By Tracy R. Twyman

ISBN: 978-1-962312-14-1

© 2007

Quintessential Publications

Contents

Hocus Pocus: The Magical Power of St. Peter

By Tracy R. Twyman

We all know that according to the Gospels, Jesus was endowed with a number of supernatural abilities, as evidenced by his many miracles. These included healing the sick, casting out demons, and raising the dead, as well as tricks like multiplying the loaves and the fishes, turning water into wine, and calming the stormy sea. This he did through the command of the so-called "Holy Spirit." This power is otherwise called, in the Gospels, his "virtue." *Luke Chapter 6:19* tells us, "And the whole multitude sought to touch him: for there went virtue out of him, and he healed all." In *Mark Chapter 5:30*, a woman does indeed touch the hem of Jesus' garment, and is immediately healed of an illness without Jesus even knowing what happened. He was only aware that someone touched him, because he felt the "virtue" leave his body. This indicates that the virtue was a supernatural agency that was always with Jesus, and which he could command, but which could also act independently of him.

Jesus' virtue seems to have come to him following his baptism by John in the Jordan river, when the "Holy Spirit" descended upon him "like a dove" and "like lightning." Jesus himself acknowledged that the "authority" by which he performed his miracles was the same authority by which John baptized people. John had the authority to command the Holy Spirit to descend upon those whom he baptized. So therefore Jesus' "virtue" was the Holy Spirit, which he had the "authority" to command after he was baptized by John.

But what specifically do we mean by the term "command the Holy Spirit"? Judaic tradition states that God himself has a secret name, and that anyone who knows how to pronounce it can command God to perform any desired miracle. According to the sixth century Jewish text *Toledoth Yeshu*, Jesus discovered the Foundation Stone of the Temple of Jerusalem, where the secret name of God was written. There was a spell on the stone that caused whoever read the name on the stone to forget it as soon as they left the temple. But Jesus jotted down the secret name on a scrap of parchment. He then cut a wound in his own thigh and concealed the parchment within it. From that moment on, the text claims, he was able to perform miracles. Although the *Toledoth Yeshu* is a biased anti-Christian text and perhaps not reliable, it does seem from the descriptions of his miracles in the Gospels that Jesus had obtained the power to command the Holy Name. But the Gospels indicate that he obtained this from John, not from a stone inside the Temple.

The Gospels also say that Jesus passed these powers onto one of his disciples, Simon, whom he renamed "Peter" ("rock"), as a metaphorical reference to the Foundation Stone of the Temple. Jesus told Peter that he would be the foundation stone of a new edifice – the church that Jesus would have him build. He specifically endowed Peter with the "keys of the kingdom of Heaven", and told him "whatsoever thou shalt bind on earth shall be bound in heaven: and whatsoever thou shalt loose on earth shall be loosed in heaven."

The "keys" being referred to here are, I believe, the letters of the secret name of God. The things that Peter was being instructed to "bind" and "loose" were spirits in Heaven. Islamic and esoteric Jewish legends state that, with the secret name of God, one can command all of the angels and demons to do one's bidding. *The Koran* even says that Adam was specifically given dominion over the angels, as well as the creatures of the Earth. According to this legend, Satan was cast from Heaven because he refused God's command for all the angels to bow down to Adam. Over the years since Adam's death, the secret of commanding the angels has been lost to all but a select few of his descendants, but it is the divine right of us all. It is the secret of pronouncing the name of God. With this, Moses parted the Red Sea, and brought plagues to Egypt. His brother Aaron unlocked the powers of the Ark of the Covenant with it. With this secret also, according to legend, King Solomon conjured up demons, which he used as workmen in the construction of his famous temple to God. This is the power that Jesus had, and which he passed on to St. Peter.

It is upon this endowment that the power of the Catholic Church was built. For Peter became the first Bishop of Rome, and the seat of the Bishop of Rome has, according the to Catholic Church's doctrine of apostolic succession, "primacy" over all Christian churches. For even the Eastern Orthodox Church, which split away from Papal dominance centuries ago, still acknowledges the "primacy" of the Bishop of Rome, although they consider it a mere "primacy of honor" and have their own tradition apart from the Church.

The tremendous accomplishments of the Catholic Church throughout history could certainly be considered evidence of the legitimacy of that dispensation, and the very real spiritual power it represents. No other institution on Earth has been so influential. For millions of people throughout the world, the pronouncements of the Church dictate the very definition of reality itself. They really believe that the Pope is infallible, and has the power to decide the post-mortal fate of all human beings on Earth. With the stroke of the Pope's pen, millions of names can be blotted from the Book of Life, ensuring eternal damnation. Or likewise, millions of souls can be relocated from Limbo to Heaven, as the Pope announced in recent years regarding the fate of infants who died without being baptized. If people are willing to believe that the Pope has this power, is it so far-fetched to believe that the Holy Father and the priests of the Catholic Church might have power over more mundane matters pertaining to life on Earth for the Church and its congregation?

Not at all. In fact, such a belief has been implicit in the doctrine of the Church since the very beginning, and even more so in the general belief of its laity. The history of Europe is rife with examples of the belief that a Catholic priest can, through prayer and ceremony, control the weather, cure illnesses, bestow blessings and remove curses upon people. This occurs more frequently in Europe's countryside, but not exclusively, and is not necessarily any less prevalent today than it was in the Middle Ages. This is based on belief in the ability of every priest ordained by the Catholic Church to perform a miracle called "Transubstantiation of the Eucharist" during the ritual of the Mass.

The origin of the word "Mass", like the ritual itself, can be found in the rites of the cult of Mithras. The Catholic Eucharist, in which bread and wine is ritually consumed, is done in commemoration of the last meal that was shared by Jesus and his disciples. Likewise, in the mystery religion of Mithraism, a ritual involving the consumption of bread and wine was celebrated in commemoration of the last meal that the legendary Mithras is said to have shared with his father-god Helios before ascending to Heaven. The bread in the Mithraic ritual was called the "mizd", a word reminiscent of the name of the Persian god Ahura-Mazda in the Zoroastrian religion, sometimes spelled "Ormuzd" or "Ormus." The word "Mazd" is the probable origin for the title of the Catholic ritual known as the "Mass", in which the Eucharist is consumed. The word is probably also related to the Jewish name for unleavened bread, "matza", which they consume ritually every Passover.

The Mithraic "Mizd" was a small round cake embossed with an equilateral cross on top. It was identical in size, shape, and ornament to the Communion wafers now used in Catholic Mass, which are small disks of unleavened bread with a cross on top. At the Last Supper, Jesus told his disciples to drink wine and eat bread "in remembrance" of him. He also said that the bread *was* his flesh, and that the wine *was* his blood. So by consuming them, Catholics believe they are becoming one with Jesus, who is himself one with God the Father. Thus the Eucharist is a sacrificial rite as well – a recreation of the ritual sacrifice of Jesus to God on the cross, laid upon the altar. It is also a way of internalizing the Holy Spirit.

Likewise, the Mithraists celebrated a similar rite wherein a bull was sacrificed. This was supposed to represent an episode in the life of Mithras. By eating the meat and drinking the blood of the sacrifice, the Mithraists believed they were becoming one with their deity. It is because the bread represents the body of the sacrifice that Catholics call it the "host", which is derived from the Latin word "hostia", meaning "sacrificial victim." It also denotes someone who is being held prisoner, which is where we get the English word "hostage." Before his execution (sacrifice), of course, Jesus was held captive. But there may be another hidden meaning as well.

In the Judaic rites that were once performed in the Tabernacle by the ancient priesthood of Aaron, burnt offerings would be sacrificed to the Lord, whose spirit would come down in a pillar of fire to consume them from the altar. This is why, during the Catholic rite of the Eucharist, the wine and bread are placed inside of a box or vessel on the altar that is called a "Tabernacle." The priests of the Israelites were able to call the spirit of God from Heaven using his secret name, so that he personally would consume the sacrifice within the sacred space of the Tabernacle. Likewise, Catholics believe that a priest actually has the authority to call Jesus down from Heaven and, within the sacred space of their Tabernacle, cause him to physically incarnate into the bread and wine. Then God - vicariously, through the priest and congregation – consumes the sacrifice of his son. Thus the priest and congregation are essentially sharing a meal with Jesus and God, just as the disciples did at the Last Supper. As the priest and congregation consume the bread and wine, the Holy Spirit enters into them.

The idea that a priest or magician can cause a spirit to enter into a physical object is an ancient one. The simplest way to think of it is to think of the Arabic legends of the genie in the lamp. A spirit can be invoked into a vessel and then controlled by the owner of the vessel, who can demand that the spirit performs miracles. This notion that the spiritual vessel can be an item of food or drink, which then causes the spirit to incarnate in the person who consumes it, is also ancient. This occurs in *The Gospel of John, Chapter 13: 26 – 27*, where Jesus invokes Satan into a piece of bread and then gives it to Judas to eat. Judas then becomes possessed by Satan and proceeds to betray Jesus.

Invoking a spirit into a vessel and then forcing it to perform miracles is indeed one of the most basic practices of witchcraft and occult practice. It is no surprise, then, that many Protestant churches and other non-Catholic Christian groups do not celebrate the Eucharist, as they believe it to be dangerously close to the practice of witchcraft, which is expressly forbidden in the Bible. In fact, the term "jack-in-the-box" was originally a derogatory term used by non-Catholics to refer to the host inside of the Tabernacle. "Jack" has for centuries been a slang term for a spirit or a demon. The term "jack-in-the-box was used by those who believed that it was a demonic spirit, and not Jesus, that was being invoked into the Communion wafer. Likewise, the term "hocus pocus", slang for magic and sorcery, is derived from the Latin words used by a priest to miraculously affect the Transubstantiation of the Host: "Hoc est corpus Jesu Christi" ("This is the body of Jesus Christ"). Then from "hocus pocus" we also get "hokum", "hokey", and "hoax."

It is legitimate, in my opinion, to say that the Catholic rite of the Eucharist parallels precisely the rituals practiced by our pagan forefathers, as well as by modern witches and ritual occultists. But so, too, apparently, were the acts of Jesus himself. He obtained mastery of the Holy Spirit through the secret name of God, then passed this power on to Peter and the Catholic Church, where mastery of the Holy Spirit is achieved through the rite of the Eucharist.

The ability to transubstantiate the Host is believed to be the power of every properly ordained priest in the Catholic Church, regardless of the personal character, faith, or spiritual alignment of that priest, just as the Pope is infallible regardless of the same. A child molester, murderer or Satanist can still make the Holy Spirit come into the Host, as long as he is an ordained Catholic priest. And the Eucharist can then be used as a vehicle for wish-fulfillment, because it is during Mass that the priest presents the deity directly with the list of blessings – a perhaps also curses – the he and his congregation wish God to bestow. This has led to numerous instances throughout history of people paying Catholic priests to perform specific masses for specific causes, to fulfill personal desires. It is no different from going to a voodoo witchdoctor and paying him to sacrifice a chicken for a love spell or a money spell. When not sanctioned by the Church, selling masses is a serious offence that falls under the category of "simony", and can cause a priest to be defrocked or even excommunicated. But over the centuries, many, many such ceremonies have been performed by Catholic priests without the sanction of the Church – not *officially*, at least.

A perfect example illustrating all of these principles is described in anthropologist Sir James Frazer's classic, *The Golden Bough*, which explores primitive concepts of magic and religion throughout the world. He writes:

> ... *French peasants used to be, perhaps are still, persuaded that the priests could celebrate, with certain special rites, a Mass of the Holy Spirit, of which the efficacy was so miraculous that it never met with any opposition from the divine will; God was forced to grant whatever was asked of Him in this form, however rash and importunate might be the petition ... in some villages, when a change of pastors takes place, the parishioners are eager to learn whether the new incumbent has the power (pouder), as they call it.*

There is no doubt that this described method whereby a priest may constrain the Holy Spirit into doing his bidding is no different than the concept of Jewish magicians constraining God with the use of the secret divine name. In this case, the Host really is a hostage! Moreover, the method and purpose of constraining God is the same as the methods used by magicians of all cultures throughout history to constrain gods, spirits, demons and elementals in order to form pacts with them. To use such a technique against God himself certainly seems impious. In some documented instances, its application has been downright diabolical.

In the same chapter that the above quotation is pulled from, James Frazer describes another unauthorized church rite called "the Mass of Saint Secaire", the purpose of which is to put a death curse on an enemy. It is supposed to be performed in a dilapidated, abandoned church at midnight. In it the regular Catholic Mass is said backwards, the Host is black, and the chalice is filled not with wine, but with "the water of a well into which the body of an unbaptized infant has been flung." When the priest makes the sign of the cross during this rite, it is upon the ground with his left foot. The victim of the curse will allegedly die of a wasting disease.

The truth is, there is no "Saint Secaire." The name appears to be related to a family of French words pertaining to dryness, barrenness, and wasting. The nature of the ceremony is most definitely evil, and it would appear that this is a form of the "Black Mass", as it has come to be known. The Black Mass is a parody of the traditional Catholic Mass wherein key elements have been altered to make the ritual blasphemous. It may involve inverted crosses, words said or actions performed in reverse (as in the Mass of Saint Secaire), and a black-colored Host that may be formed with human body fluids or other disgusting substances. The words of the Mass may be altered to include blasphemies against God and Jesus, or praise of Satan. The rite may include sexual acts, and is traditionally performed with the stomach of a naked woman used as the altar. The consecrated Host may be abused or humiliated, as though the priest were actually doing these things to Jesus himself, who is incarnated in the Host. Demons are evoked and, perhaps most horrible of all, unbaptized infants are sacrificed, their blood used instead of the wine of the Eucharist. But the purpose of the ritual is to force God to constrain the invoked demons to fulfill the priest's requests, and the sacrifices are made to God in exchange for that, not to the demons.

The elements of the Black Mass are identical in many ways to the elements of the alleged "Witch's Sabbath" that convicted witches have confessed to attending throughout the centuries of Christian persecution of said witches. From the Middle Ages of Europe, to sixteenth century England, to colonial America, the descriptions of the Witch's Sabbath in these confessions are remarkably uniform. In these ceremonies, officiated by the Devil himself, there was a mock Eucharist with a black Host, blaspheming of God, and ritual trampling upon the Cross. New initiates were made to sign a black book pledging their soul to the Devil, and they received a mark from the Devil that tagged them as belonging to him. The main difference between the Witch's Sabbath and the Black Mass is that the Sabbath is a Satanic rite in homage to the Devil, whereas the Black Mass is a Christian rite performed for evil purposes. Sabbaths were sometimes, but not always, performed with the help of an ordained Catholic priest. But Black Masses were, by definition, always performed by a real Catholic priest. Although the descriptions of the Witch's Sabbaths were extracted under torture, and may be considered untrustworthy because the trials were part of a campaign of persecution against certain groups of non-Catholics, the Church would seemingly have no reason to accuse its own priests of performing such blasphemous rites, unless it were undeniably true. Yet the fact remains that throughout history, more than a few respected priests have confessed to performing the Black Mass, including the sacrifice of children.

The history of the Black Mass begins with the case of Catherine de Medici, queen consort of King Henry II of France from 1547 to 1559. She was born into an influential noble family that had provided the world with two Popes and numerous noble figures. They had a tremendous influence upon the spread of Humanist philosophy, art and science throughout Renaissance Europe. But they were also known for being dabblers in the occult. Catherine de Medici's sons were heirs to the throne, and she herself was appointed regent for a time. According to French political writer Jean Bodin, Catherine attempted to prolong the life of her son Philip, who was dying of a wasting disease, by employing a priest to perform black masses that involved the murder of young boys. Catherine is known to have worn a magical amulet featuring the sigil of the demon Asmodeus. Her son, Henry III, continued her interest in the Dark Arts, and had an altar in his home that featured cloven-hoofed devils bearing their backsides to the Cross.

Catherine de Medici was never convicted of child murder, blasphemy or witchcraft, and in fact, these stories about her are rarely mentioned by modern historians, although they were widely believed at the time. But in the famous case of the Abbe Guiborg and Catherine Deshayes (La Voison), mistress to King Louis XIV, the perpetrators were actually brought to justice. The mistress hired the Abbe to perform hundreds of black masses in which the demon Asmodeus was invoked and children were sacrificed. La Voison herself acted as the naked female altar in these ceremonies, and after the child was slain, the blood would be poured into the ceremonial chalice. The host would be inserted into La Voison's vagina during consecration, instead of the traditional "Tabernacle." Afterwards, the Abbe and La Voison would engage in sex acts, then the fluids would be mixed in with the blood and the foully consecrated host. This mixture was then surreptitiously added to the King's food, the purpose being to cause him to continue to love La Voison to the exclusion of all others, including his wife. This is all according to both Deshayes and Guiborg's confessions at the trial, and the documentary evidence, in the form of signed demonic pacts between La Voison and Asmodeus, which were entered as evidence in the trial.

That a consecrated wafer could be used for black magic of this sort is a common theme in European occultism. In his famous novel dealing with the Black Mass, French writer J.K. Huysmans wrote in his 1891 book *The Damned* about a method of killing one's enemies performed by certain priests in Paris. The priest would put small, non-lethal amounts of poisonous substances onto consecrated wafers, and feed them to either a human female or an animal. After the wafers had been digested, blood would be taken from them – menstrual blood in the case of the human female. The priest would then conjure a demon, and instruct the demon to deliver the blood to the intended victim as a poison.

It is unclear to this author how this process is any easier, or preferable, to poisoning someone outright, except that it can be done from a distance with a much smaller chance of getting caught or prosecuted for murder, but presumably a much lower rate of success. Perhaps, if you are a diabolically-minded priest with God-ordained authority over the spirit world, you find conjuring a demon to be simpler than organizing a murder conspiracy. But if you can do that, why not just ask the demon to kill the person for you through magic? Why would you create a material poison and then ask an ethereal agent to deliver it? I must admit I don't really get it myself. But it is interesting that Communion wafers were considered to be required for this spell to work. This brings to mind the fact that Catherine de Medici was suspected of poisoning several of her enemies to death, but no one could ever prove it was her who had done it. Perhaps she had demons deliver the poisons? Perhaps the poisons were made with consecrated hosts?

The demand for transubstantiated wafers has always been high amongst practitioners of black magic, according to Montague Summers' 1946 book *Witchcraft and Black Magic*. Unscrupulous people looking to make a buck on the black market will, they say, preserve the host under their tongue after Communion at church, then take it out and sell it to the highest bidder. Ebay has officially banned the sale of consecrated hosts after someone tried to list one for auction, and the company received 9000 complaints from outraged Catholics. To a truly believing Catholic, letting unbelievers get hold of a consecrated Host is like letting Hitler get hold of the Holy Grail. It has transcendental power that can be used for good or for evil, and in the wrong hands could potentially be used against the Church's interests.

I mentioned earlier the Catholic doctrine that Jesus appointed St. Peter to be the founder of his church, and gave to Peter the keys to Heaven, bestowing power over the spiritual destinies of men, and over the spirits in the ether. The legitimacy of this dispensation is one apparently recognized by even the heretics of the Catholic tradition. Peter was the first Pope. Via what is called "chirothesy" or "the laying on of hands", Peter was able to ordain other bishops to help lead the church in various areas, and passed the power down to them as well. ("Chirothesy" was also used by Popes to heal the sick.) These priests in turn passed the power on to other priests that they ordained, and the pattern has continued to the present day. Thus, via apostolic succession, there is a vast web of interweaving but unbroken lines of spiritual power which have been transmitted from Jesus, through Saint Peter, down to all of the validly ordained bishops of the present day. The term "validly ordained" does not necessarily mean "orthodox", as I shall explain.

Once a spiritual dispensation has been accepted by the Church as valid, it is all but impossible to revoke. Thus we have the phenomenon of "wandering bishops", and the offshoot Catholic churches that trace their origin through them. These are churches begun by validly ordained Catholic bishops that have broken away from some of the teachings of the Roman church, and from the direct control of the Pope. However, they nonetheless practice Catholic rites and consider themselves to be under the Catholic fold, tracing their apostolic succession back to Peter through the Roman Church. Some of the oldest such churches include the Dutch Old Catholic Church, the Old Catholic Church in Great Britain, and the Liberal Catholic Church. Strangely, the legitimacy of these churches is mutually, if begrudgingly, acknowledged by the Holy See, in much the same way that the Eastern Orthodox Church is acknowledged, although these other churches are very small and considered unimportant. According to the "doctrine of orders", expounded by St. Augustine, apostolic succession by the laying-on of hands is valid regardless of the relative orthodoxy or heterodoxy of the recipient's religious beliefs.

What is interesting is that many of these break-off churches have become intertwined with the underground network of occult secret societies throughout the world. Several of them teach Gnosticism, and act as the "ecclesiastical bodies" for groups like the Ordo Templi Orientis and the Golden Dawn. One such group is attached to a modern-day Templar order that claims to be a legitimate continuation of the original. The thing is that these occult groups not only teach heresy, but outright blasphemy. Indeed, their teachings could be considered Luciferian in nature, and several of the founders of these groups were openly Luciferian or Satanist. These same people are attending Catholic masses performed by priests who trace their apostolic succession back to legitimately ordained bishops. So once again we have Satanists and occultists deliberately utilizing the power of St. Peter for purposes that could by considered anti-Christian.

But interestingly, this seems to be how a lot of the heresies persecuted by the Catholic Church have begun: within the Church itself. Take, for instance, the Cathar heresy, against which the Church waged a Crusade in Southern France in the thirteenth century. This was a Catholic Gnostic movement being led by duly ordained Catholic priests. It is in fact *because* they were part of the Catholic Church that they were called "heretics." Otherwise, they would merely be "heathen." The Church persecuted heresy with much greater vehemence than they did mere unbelief, for heresy was much more threatening. But in more recent years, the Church has been unable to persecute heretics at all, and thus these heretical but nonetheless legitimate bishoprics have proliferated.

It has been suggested by authors like Dr. Margaret Alice Murray, and more recently Nicholas de Vere, that most of the accused witches were prosecuted specifically for "heresy", and thus were practicing a form of heretical Christianity, be it pagan or overtly Satanic in form. One group of witches, prosecuted in Aberdeen, Scotland, even confessed that they called the god they worshipped "Christsonday" (or "Christ, Son Dei", meaning, "Christ, Son of God"). However, their description of Christsonday seemed to match the Christian devil much more than that of Jesus. Nicholas de Vere takes this to a further conclusion, stating in his book *The Dragon Legacy* that:

> "Witchcraft in Europe and Britain was run by the Templars and Cathars ... Witchcraft is original Christianity, practicing Christian Gnostic Dualism ... [It can be traced] back through the Templars to Jesus' original teachings and the culture of the Druids. ... Witchcraft proper, from the early Dark Ages onwards owes as much to its clearly Christian as it does to its direct Druidic, origins ... the Roman church ... sanitized [Jesus'] rituals and concealed his descent. All those who continued to follow Jesus' original teachings – like the witches – [the Catholic Church] burned as 'heretics'... To call a witch a heretic meant that the witch was a heterodox Christian... Witches were 'original Christians' whose knowledge of the true, Druidic nature of Jesus' liberating Christianity had to be quashed at any cost if the Church were to achieve the political and pecuniary supremacy they desired by replacing it with their own enslaving dogma."

In De Vere's worldview, the Black Mass is:

"...the original mass of Jesus which the Catholics later stole and sanitized for public consumption.... The Black Mass had its roots in the ancient alchemical lore of Solomon and was simply a memento of teachings long past and an aide memoire for future generations..."

The "Black Mass" which De Vere is here referring to here, performed by witches in Britain and Europe for centuries, is one in which menstrual blood is consumed at the Eucharist, not the blood of sacrificed infants, and has nothing to do with abusing consecrated wafers or calling God nasty names, like in the Black Masses of De Medici or La Voison. Nonetheless, the existence of beliefs like those quoted above may explain why occultists and Satanists might still consider themselves Christians and respect the Catholic Church.

Moreover, occultists are always looking for a greater source of spiritual energy to power their rituals. Occult magicians operate using what they call "magical currents." Any individual can make a personal pact with a spiritual entity and receive a dispensation of spiritual power from that entity, which that person can then use to energize their magic rituals. But if you belong to a magical order, you can partake of the spiritual dispensation which that group has already obtained, based on a pact negotiated by the founders of the group with that group's patron deity. This spiritual dispensation becomes a power base that can be used by all of the members of the group, perhaps to varying degrees according to rank, and it can be transmitted to others in a manner similar to apostolic succession in the Catholic Church. This line of power transmission is a "magical current."

When new occult groups spring up, they always claim to trace their lineage of spiritual authority back to some other important group, like the Knights Templar, so that they can utilize that group's magical current. Within the modern Gnostic Catholic churches and the occult orders that are attached to them, it is clear that they see apostolic succession from Saint Peter as the ultimate magical current, and they believe that they are tapped into it directly. C.W. Leadbeater,

Theosophist and founder of the Liberal Catholic Church, wrote:

> *"When the great World-Teacher [Jesus] was last on earth, He made a special arrangement that what we may think of as a compartment of a reservoir of spiritual power should be available for the use of the new religion that he founded, and that its officials should be empowered, by the use of certain ceremonies, words, and signs of power, to draw upon it for the spiritual benefit of their people."*

This expression is not dissimilar to the way that the Catholic Church itself views the power of St. Peter. The Church has utilized all of the tried and true methods used by history's most successful religious cults to create the greatest spiritual power base the world has ever known. As I explained in my book *Solomon's Treasure: The Magic and Mystery of America's Money* (Dragon Key Press, 2005), the Catholic Church is organized into what I call a "spiritual pyramid scheme" that acts as a magical energy multiplier. This is the way all cults, secret societies, fraternities and similar institutions operate. It starts with a pact formed between the founders of the institution and its patron deity – in this case, between Simon Peter and Jesus Christ. A magical current of spiritual power, and the authority to utilize it, is bestowed by the deity upon the leadership of the institution. The laity of the institution is then able to partake of the benefits of these blessings, including the right to have their prayers heard and desires fulfilled by the deity, in this case, via the priests, the Pope, and the Saints. In return they must give one or more forms of spiritual energy to the institution, which can include faith, love, sacrifices, tithes, etc. The spiritual energy from these gifts is then channeled back to the deity, again via the priests, the Pope, and the Saints. As this energy moves through the system, it is multiplied exponentially at each step, strengthening the institution as a whole, much like money moving through a nation's economy.

Part of what has made the Church such a powerful energy multiplier is that it was built upon the foundation of a powerful institution - the state-run priesthood of the Roman Empire – and absorbed the power of other cults throughout the world as it grew. Christianity was first named an official religion in Rome during the reign of Emperor Constantine. This man was allegedly converted to Christianity by an apparition of Jesus, but still remained loyal to the pagan cult of Sol Invictus (the Sun), which he had recently been initiated into just prior to his famous religious vision. It seems that he was simultaneously both a Christian and a sun-worshipper, and apparently didn't see any inherent conflict there. This man is so important to the birth of the Catholic Church that he is called the "Thirteenth Apostle", and his mother Helena (also both a Christian and a sun-worshipper), was responsible for "discovering" a number of key relics related to Jesus in the Holy Land, such as the "True Cross." What that really means is that she was responsible for deciding which relics of Jesus would be named as such, and what areas in the Holy Land would be designated as sacred shrines. It was during Constantine's reign, and at his urging, that the Council of Nicaea met to decide the nature of Jesus' divinity, and other key tenets of what is now Christian orthodoxy. Their decisions formed the building blocks of what is now the canonized Bible and the Catholic Church.

So what has been the influence of two pagan sun-worshippers, Constantine and Helena, on the foundation of Catholicism in Rome? While Christ-centered and strongly colored by Judaic theology, Catholicism is nonetheless constructed with ritual elements that are entirely pagan and/or pre-Christian. This subject has been discussed exhaustively by many previous authors, but for the sake of continuity I will mention some of the key points.

As the Catholic Church built its foundations and spread its influence about the world, it went about co-opting the mythologies, gods, feast-days, symbols, and ritual elements of other religions, just as the Roman Empire had done before as it spread itself through conquest. It was by amalgamating the conquered cultures with its own that the Roman Empire achieved its greatness, and the Roman Church did likewise. So the Catholics co-opted December 25th, the "Natalis Invictus", or "day of the rebirth of the Sun", from Constantine's cult of Sol Invictus, and turned it into Christmas. Easter was rightly tied to Passover, as the Passion of Christ had taken place at that time, but the Christian celebration of Christ's death and resurrection was modeled after the pagan festival of the Spring Equinox. Even the Jewish Sabbath day, considered so sacred that those caught violating its taboos could be killed on sight, was "re-consecrated" by the Catholics and switched to Sunday, literally the traditional day for the pagan worship of the Sun.

The symbols used in the church's icons all bear resemblance to those of the ancient world. The image of the Virgin Mary holding the child Jesus is always presented in a manner almost identical to images of Ishtar and Tammuz from Babylon, or Isis and Horus in Egypt. The presentation of the Virgin Mary in particular is unmistakably copied from that of Ishtar or Isis, the main goddess of the ancient world, called "Venus" by the Romans. She was named the "Queen of Heaven" by the ancients, and shown with a crown of stars around her head, and a crescent moon beneath her feet. The same images and title are associated with Mary in Catholic iconography. Likewise, Ishtar's son, the sun God incarnated as a man, was presented the same way in the ancient world as Jesus has been presented by the Catholic church. Like the sun god, he is said to have died, descended to the Underworld, and risen alive three days later. Like the sun god, Jesus is shown with a sun-disk-shaped halo around his head. The cross associated with Jesus was a symbol of the sun in the ancient world too. This is what is called "iconotropy", defined as "the accidental or deliberate misinterpretation by one culture of the icons or myths of an earlier one, especially so as to bring them into accord with those of the later one"

The offices of the church were likewise modeled after ancient prototypes. The official title of the Pope – Pontifex Maximus (meaning "great bridge-builder") was the same title used by the high priest of the state cult of the old Roman Empire. Like the eunuch priests of ancient Babylon, Catholic priests wear black and observe celibacy. As the ancient world had vestal virgins draped in black, symbolizing their mourning of the death of the sun God, the Catholic Church has nuns pledged to celibacy.

The vow of poverty observed by priests, nuns and monks is an ancient tradition too, observed by the priests of Babylon, Rome, and ancient Israel. In any spiritual pyramid scheme, money is a form of energy given to the institution by its members, and it is customary that the custodians of the institution should not profit from that money directly like the owners of a business would, but rather should only benefit from it indirectly. The money tithed to the Church by its members is considered to be a sacrifice given to God, for the maintenance of His church, and the maintenance of the daily needs of the priesthood just happens to be part of that. The priests are considered to be mere instruments in the machinery of the pyramid scheme, the purpose of which is to channel spiritual energy to God, and to multiply that energy as efficiently as possible through that machinery.

In the beginning, whenever the Catholics built a new church or cathedral, it was usually upon the foundations of an old pagan temple. Sometimes they would simply re-consecrate an existing shrine or temple and alter the interior decoration. Even the Church's global headquarters, the Vatican, is the site of an old Roman oracle of the same name, and the name literally means "serpent of divination." Each new Catholic Church was dedicated to a particular "saint." A saint is usually a deceased person who the Church has officially "consecrated" and raised to a status resembling that of a demi-god of the pagan world. The saints act as intercessors between the living Catholics and their God. People can pray to the saints and ask the saints to pray to God for them on their behalf. The saint most commonly prayed to in this manner is "Saint Mary, Mother of God", i.e. the Virgin Mary.

Each saint has particular attributes that define the nature of their spiritual power, like gods of the ancient world, and each sphere of existence has its own "patron saint", like pagans had "patron deities" for each area of life. So there is a patron saint of doctors, another for travelers, a patron saint of "lost causes", and a patron saint of basketball. In many cases, the attributes of saints can be traced directly to a pagan god with similar attributes, as if the pagan god had been merely "re-consecrated" by the church, given a new name and incorporated into Christianity. Sometimes the new name is almost identical to the old one, as in the case of St. Bridget and the Celtic goddess Brighid. St. Briget's feast day even falls on that of her pagan predecessor, February 1, called "Imbolg" by the Celts. St. Denis, who allegedly walked around holding his own decapitated head before he died, is probably modeled on the Greek God Dionysus, who had a similar episode in his mythical life. Likewise Saints Hermes and Mercury were probably named after the Greek and Roman gods, respectively.

Many times a new church, built upon the ruins of a pagan temple, would be dedicated to the very saint who had replaced that temple's patron pagan god in the Catholic pantheon. In some cases it is doubtful that there ever was a real living human that the saint was based on – as in the case of St. Christopher, a mythical giant whom the Church itself now acknowledges was never an actual person. The saints were merely characters concocted to replace the pagan gods whom the Church had co-opted into their own spiritual power structure. In the Caribbean, this practice lent itself to the development of Santeria, in which the identities of Christian saints were transposed onto those of traditional African gods. Thus the African slaves taken to these islands were able to continue practicing voodoo with a Christian veneer. Santeria is a very powerful system of ritual magic that remains popular among native Caribbeans and Western occultists to this very day.

One has to understand that the Church's tactics here were not used merely for political expediency, to make the new religion more palatable to converts, or because the church leaders were too unimaginative to come up with new symbols. There are very old, very powerful spiritual concepts at work here. In the ancient world, when one culture would take over another through military conquest, the conquered culture's gods would be conquered as well – literally, in a spiritual way. Like the god of the Hebrews, many gods of the ancients had a secret name, and it was believed that anyone who knew that name could control them. So when taking over another people's gods, it was important to extract from their priests the secret names of those gods. Then you could rededicate them, give them new names, and incorporate them into your own cult, making them subservient to your own gods. As Robert Graves writes in *The White Goddess*:

> *"In ancient times, once a god's secret name had been discovered, the enemies of his people could do destructive magic against them with it. The Romans made a regular practice of discovering the secret names of enemy gods and summoning them to Rome with seductive promises, a process technically known as* elicio...*Naturally, the Romans, like the Jews, hid the secret name of their own guardian deity with extraordinary care."*

So like the Roman Empire before them, the Catholic Church conquered all of the gods of the world's pagan cults, and incorporated them as saints, putting them under the command of Jesus, and plugging these existing magical currents into the energy multiplier of the Church. This is wholly appropriate, for the belief system espoused by Jesus himself was a conglomeration of Judaic mysticism, Greek mystery religions, Zoroastrianism, and many other ideas. This tradition has been inherited, and is being continued in spirit by the Catholic Church, which styles itself the "Universal Church" ("universal" being the meaning of the word "Catholic"). Just as the Romans "Hellenized" the world, the Church has Catholicized the world. This is why the Church literally tries to be all things to all people. That's why it is actually loathe to excommunicate heretics, preferring to keep renegade churches under the fold rather than force orthodoxy on them and risk losing them. The Church is a machine built for the purpose of amassing as much spiritual power as possible. Ultimately, it would like to control all spiritual power that there is in Heaven and on Earth. This includes incorporating every single demi-god or demon as a saint, and commanding the worship of every human being on Earth.

Earlier I hypothesized about the origin of the word "Mass" used in regards to the Catholic ritual of that name. I traced it back to the rites of Mithraism, where the Eucharistic bread was called the "Mizd." But in English, "mass" is also a word that means "conglomerate, coagulate, combine, or come together." In a way, that is what happens at a Catholic Mass: the laity and the priesthood all come together and commune with their god and the saints. That is why the Eucharist is also called "Communion." Interestingly, there is another piece of Catholic terminology which is related to this concept. It is called the "Communion of Saints." The online Catholic Encyclopedia defines it thusly:

> *"The communion of saints is the spiritual solidarity which binds together the faithful on earth, the souls in purgatory, and the saints in heaven in the organic unity of the same mystical body under Christ its head, and in a constant interchange of supernatural offices. The participants in that solidarity are called saints by reason of their destination and of their partaking of the fruits of the Redemption* (1 Corinthians 1:2 &151; Greek Text). *The damned are thus excluded from the communion of saints. The living, even if they do not belong to the body of the true Church, share in it according to the measure of their union with Christ and with the soul of the Church. St. Thomas [Aquinas] teaches (III:8:4) that the angels, though not redeemed, enter the communion of saints because they come under Christ's power and receive of His* gratia capitis. *The solidarity itself implies a variety of inter-relations: within the Church Militant, not only the participation in the same faith, sacraments, and government, but also a mutual exchange of examples, prayers, merits, and satisfactions; between the Church on earth on the one hand, and purgatory and heaven on the other, suffrages, invocation, intercession, veneration.*

This term "gratia capitis," was coined by St. Thomas Aquinas and means "the sanctifying grace of Christ the Head (the new Adam) that flows in plenitude over the elect." This is the power of the Holy Spirit, the power Jesus claimed when he commanded the secret name of God, and the power he passed down to St. Peter. This definition of the Communion of Saints is an exact description of how the Catholic Church acts as a spiritual energy multiplier, exchanging energy between God, Jesus, the Saints, the angels, the priests, the dead laity in Heaven and the living laity on Earth.

Throughout its history, the Church has tried to amass as much spiritual power as possible by re-baptizing the gods of the old world as saints and binding them to the command of the church with the name of Jesus Christ. The rights given to St. Peter by Jesus said that "whatever he "binds" on Earth will be bound in Heaven, and whatever he "looses" on Earth will be loosed in Heaven. What this means is that he has the power to command the spirits, the demons, and the angels, to bind them to his will and force them to do his bidding; to imprison them in Hell, or to cast them into a herd of swine, or to unleash them onto the world.

This is what the magical motto "solve et coagula", used by modern occultists, means: "dissolve and coagulate", or rather "bind and loose." This is connected to the meaning behind the Roman word for priest: "pontiff", meaning "bridge-builder." His job is to connect people with God and with the saints, to build a bridge between this world and the Otherworld. It is the duty of the Church, and the Pontifex Maximus at the helm, to build bridges between members of the laity as well, especially between people of different cultures. Since a "culture", as the root meaning of the word implies, is heavily influenced by the leading "cult" or religion observed by its people, this requires the Church to incorporate the gods of other cults into its own fold.

The Bible prophecies that "every knee shall bend" and acknowledge Jesus as Christ Lord (*Romans 14:11*, Philippians 2:10). This includes all the spirits in Heaven, on Earth, and in Hell. When the three magi came to bow down before the infant Jesus, it represented the gods of the ancient world and their priests making themselves subservient to their new master, the Christ. Just as an occult magician might impose a pact upon a demon, forcing him to grant the wishes of himself or the members of his cult when certain rituals are performed, or magic words uttered, the Church has forced a similar pact upon the gods of the ancient world, who have been re-consecrated as saints and made servitors of Jesus. They are now obligated to listen to the prayers of the Church laity, and to pass those prayers onto god, especially if the prayer is in regards to the sphere of influence that the particular saint has been assigned. Just like in ritual magic, both ancient and modern, special phrases like Hail Marys and Our Fathers can be uttered by the Church members to obtain instantaneous spiritual boons.

Many of the ritual activities of the Church resemble outright the practices of ritual magic, even though this has been expressly outlawed in the scriptures as idolatry and worship of false gods. Let's face it: Catholics are literally praying to statues that they believe to be possessed with the spirits of dead people who have obtained semi-divine status after death. That in itself is nothing less than necromancy, specifically forbidden by the scriptures in *Chronicles 10:13* and *1 Samuel 28:7*. But it is more than just necromancy, because though they may not realize it, these people are also praying to the pagan gods that those saints represent.

Elements of necromancy are at work also in the use of holy relics by the Church. These are generally the bones and other body parts believed to have belonged to saints, or even to Jesus himself. There was once a rule that no Catholic church or place or worship could be built unless there was a holy relic to associate it with. The relics would be either buried beneath the church in the crypt, or placed inside the altar, or put on display somewhere within the building. The church would then be dedicated to the saint associated with the relic, or even to the relic itself. This is rather like the ancient practice of burying the body of a sacrificed child or animal in the foundation of a new building, so that its spirit will hallow the structure. As I said before, many of the Church's earliest acquired relics were discovered by Constantine's mother Helena, including the so-called "Passion Relics" such as the True Cross and the Crown of Thorns. There is no doubt that Helena would have understood the occult implications of using relics to sanctify a church. It is quire possible that some of the relics she "discovered" were actually sacred relics of a pre-Christian origin that were then "re-consecrated" by the Church like everything else.

The use of repetitive prayer to God, Jesus and the Saints is something that resembles pagan worship and ritual magic as well, and is also expressly forbidden by Jesus. (*Matthew 6:7*: "Use not vain repetitions, as the heathen [do].") Repetitive prayer, called "chanting" outside of the Church, is one of the more basic elements of occult practice. Chanting can be used to invoke or evoke spirits, to make something supernatural happen (as magic words are used), or to put the person praying in an alternate state of consciousness. The vast majority of these prayers or chants by Catholics are actually addressed to the Virgin, who has been named the official intercessor of record charged with forwarding prayer requests from the faithful to Jesus her son. None can honestly claim that the Church does not honor the "sacred feminine principle", for the Virgin, a replacement for the mother goddess of the ancients, is revered by the Catholics seemingly even more so that Jesus himself. There is even a word for this cult worship of the Virgin: "Mariology."

The most common prayer to Mary is the "Ave Maria" or "Hail Mary", which consists of five lines requesting Mary to "pray for us sinners, now, and at the hour of our death." A series of Hail Marys may be assigned to a sinner at Confession, with the confessor assured by the priest that saying X number of these prayers will absolve whatever sins were confessed. A program requiring the repetition of 150 Hail Marys, called the "rosary", is used quite often by Catholics. The prayers are broken down into sets of repetitions, and during each set the person praying is supposed to contemplate one of several specific "mysteries" in the life and death of Christ. This means literally visualizing and meditating upon these scenes while praying. A necklace of "rosary beads" can be used to count the prayers as they are repeated, and thus to keep track of where one is in the program.

Guided visions along with chanting are tactics used frequently in the practice of occult ritual magic. The origin of rosary beads goes back to ancient Rome, where a "florilgeum" was a collection of flowers, each representing a prayer to a god. A "rosarium" was a garland of such flowers, shown around the neck of the goddess Aphrodite (i.e. Venus, Isis or Ishtar, the goddess on whom the Virgin Mary's iconography is based). In the Catholic rosary, each Hail Mary is a "rose", for each has five sentences, representing the five petals on a rose, and also representing the five letters of the name "Maria." So like Aphrodite before her, the Virgin is now represented by a rose. Each bead in the rosary is a "rose" – that is, a Hail Mary – and so every time you say one, you count one bead.

The repetition of prayers, the worship of idols, the use of holy relics for necromancy, and the pagan-inspired Eucharist, with its magical transmutation of bread and wine into flesh and blood, are not the only practices of Catholics that resemble the practices of occult ritual magic and paganism. The truth is that the same could be said about virtually every aspect of Catholic ritual: kneeling and clasping hands in prayer, burning incense, the lighting of special candles, baptism, and everything else has been part of worship in every pagan culture, and also in modern ritual magic, since the beginning of history. This is why Christian groups that were formed outside of the Catholic Church, or that broke away from it, sometimes teach that the Catholic Church is a tool of the Devil, the cradle of the Anti-Christ, and the abominable Whore of Babylon prophesied in *The Revelation of St. John the Divine*. Some even claim that the use by the Church of the inverted cross – called the "Cross of St. Peter" – is evidence for the hidden Satanic nature of the Church, since inverted crosses were used in the Black Mass as an insult to Christ. (Really, it just symbolizes Peter's martyrdom, since he died hanging upside-down on a cross.)

Interestingly, in the General Catechism used by the Church, the Ten Commandments are presented with the second commandment – the one against worshipping graven images – actually omitted, and what is traditionally the tenth commandment is split into two parts to make a total of ten. This editing job certainly seems an attempt to distract attention away from the fact that the second commandment expressly forbids the very activity most commonly practiced by members of the Church – the worship of statues!

As an expert on the occult who believes that it really is possible to contact demonic spirits with ritual magic, I can tell you that the rosary is very much an occult ritual, and the idea of millions of believers doing it in perfect faith every day, conjuring up all that spiritual power from the ether, is enough to make the hairs on my neck stand up. A truly believing member of the Church laity can work quite powerful magic just through prayers and devotions. Imagine what a priest, endowed with the power of the Holy Spirit from St. Peter could do. Imagine what wonders the Pope himself could work, with all of his spiritual authority.

These are points that have not escaped the notice of previous Popes, some of whom have consciously attempted to use the power of the sacraments, and the authority of the papal office to perform magic. Popes that have been accused of practicing witchcraft during their reigns include Sylvester II, John XXI, Benedict IX, Benedict XII, Gregory VII, Clement IV, Boniface VIII, and Honorius III. To the latter was attributed the authorship of a grimoire which exists in several versions, written specifically for use by Catholic priests, with the purpose of evoking and controlling demons. That the grimoire was actually written by Pope Honorius is doubtful. It was, however, first published in 1670, right around the same time that La Voison and Abbe Guiborg were on trial for murdering children at black masses. Apparently many priests at this time were using the power of St. Peter for dark purposes. The attitude displayed in the introduction to *The Constitution of Pope Honorius the Great* says it all:

> "The Holy Apostolic Chair unto which the keys of the Kingdom of Heaven were given by those words that Christ Jesus addressed to St. Peter: I give unto thee the keys of the kingdom of Heaven, and unto thee alone the power of commanding the Prince of Darkness and his angels, who, as slaves of their master, do we owe him honor, glory, and obedience... hence by the power of these Keys the Head of the Church has been made the Lord of Hell."

The introduction then says that the power of commanding spirits, which had heretofore been the privileged possession of the papacy, was now going to be shared with the rest of the priesthood. The grimoire then continues, with spells typical of all magical books, for the obtainment of money, sex, invisibility, and the like. Clearly, there were several priests at this time – enough to warrant the publication of this book - who felt that the power vested in them as priests gave them the right to command the demons of the netherworld.

The spells in the grimoires of Honorius invoke the name of Jesus in order to command the demons in the same way that Jesus allegedly used the secret name of God to perform miracles. Indeed, the Church has always taught that priests could control demons, for what else is happening during an official Church-sanctioned exorcism? Here the priest commands the demon, in the name of Jesus, to leave the body of the afflicted, binds it in spiritual chains and consigns it once again to the pits of Hell. Jesus did likewise when confronted with people possessed by demons, using the Secret Name. Now the Catholic priesthood uses the name of Jesus as their word of power. Maybe there is some secret aspect to it known only to the Pope?

On this note, there is allegedly a secret passed down from one Pope to the next, which is written on a scrap of paper that is kept in a locked box. The key to that box is given to every new Pope as he is ordained. He uses it to unlock the box, alone, and reads the secret inside, only once. The box is then locked up again until the next Pope is elected. Perhaps the secret has to do with a sacred word of spiritual command known only to the Pope!

Whether or not there is any truth to that speculation, it is clear that the priesthood of the Church operates in a manner similar to the operations of modern occult magicians, and also that here are a number of occultists who have worked within the priesthood of the Church. It is for obvious reasons, then, that the Church has acquired the world's largest collection of occult-related literature and ancient religious texts. This library, part of the notorious "secret Vatican archives", is not for public consumption, again for obvious reasons. It is for obvious reasons, then, that there have been no shortage of conspiracies throughout history where occult groups have attempted to infiltrate and control the papacy from within. No power on Earth has ever been so highly prized.

One such conspiracy was that of Adam Weishaupt's Illuminati, a group held responsible for the anti-religious excesses of the French Revolution. The Illuminati was created within the ranks of Freemasonry, an occult fraternity which the church has always held with distrust, and at times forbidden its members to join. Freemasonry is the spiritual inheritance of the Knights Templar, a group of monks that the Church found threatening and persecuted on charges of witchcraft. In Italy during the 70s and 80s, a Masonic group called Propaganda Due attempted to infiltrate the upper echelons of the Church for criminal purposes, and was successful at placing its men at the helm of the Vatican Bank. The Priory of Sion, another offshoot of the Freemasons and the Knights Templar, proclaimed itself a "Catholic chilvalric order", and hinted in its press releases that it intended to take over the papacy. Pope John XXIII was even rumored to be under the Priory's control, and it was his influence that brought the end of the traditional Latin Mass in favor of the new, modern "Novus Ordo Mass." According to some alarmists, it was when the Mass was altered that Satan officially took over the Catholic Church.

Controversial cleric Malachi Martin, an exorcist and close confidant of Pope Paul II, wrote several books warning of a conspiracy of Satanic priests within the Church. He claimed personal knowledge of priests who worshipped Satan and practiced witchcraft sitting in the highest offices of the Church. He called this cabal the "Superforce." He said that they protect each other and work for each other's advancement within the Church. The priest pedophilia epidemic was directly related to this, he said, as many of the Satanist priests were pedophiles who abused children during their rituals. This was the subject of William H. Kennedy's 2005 book *Lucifer's Lodge: Satanic Ritual Abuse in the Catholic Church.*

There is no telling to what extent the so-called "Superforce" is really in charge of the Church right now, or even if such a thing truly exists. However, there can be no doubt that the Church has created the most powerful spiritual pyramid scheme the world has even seen, by taking the gods of the old world and putting them under the command of the name of Jesus. So all of the old pagan gods, supposedly the former tools of Satan, are now the tools of Christ and his Church. But what of Satan himself? He still reigns in Hell, according to the Church's own doctrine, and still wields a great deal of influence on earth. There is no doubt that the Catholic Church is the one power that Satan and his followers would most want to get their hands on. Then they could re-consecrate the Church and all of its saints in the name of the Devil. What then would happen to all of the souls who have pledged themselves to the Church? What if – God forbid – this has already happened? What if the devout Catholics of the world are already giving all of their prayers and tithes to Satan?

Perhaps it's best not to think too much about these things, especially since – thank Heaven – I'm not Catholic.

References:

Baigent, Michael, Leigh, Richard, and Lincoln, Henry. *The Messianic Legacy*. New York, NY, USA 1986.

Black, S. Jason. and Hyatt, Christopher S. *Pacts with the Devil: A Chronicle of Sex, Blasphemy and Liberation*. Phoenix, AZ, USA, 1973

The Catholic Encyclopedia, http://www.newadvent.org/cathen/ (2005.)

De Vere, Nicholas. *The Dragon Legacy: The Secret History of an Ancient Bloodline*. San Diego, CA, USA, 2004.

Frazer, Sir James George. *The Golden Bough*. New York, NY, USA, 1958.

Gest, Kevin L. *The Secrets of Solomon's Temple: Discover the Hidden Truch That Lies at the Heart of Freemasonry*. Gloucester, MA, USA, 2007.

Graves, Robert. The White Goddess: A Historical Grammar of Poetic Myth. New York, NY, USA, 1975.

Stephan A. Hoeller. "Wandering Bishops: Not All Roads Lead to Rome", *Gnosis: A Journal of Western Inner Traditions* (Vol. 12, Summer 1989), USA.

The Holy Bible: King James Version. Grand Rapids, MI, USA, 1989.

Huysmans, J. – K. The Damned. London, UK, 2001

Kennedy, William H. *Lucifer's Lodge: Satanic Ritual Abuse in the Catholic Church*. South Egremont, MA, USA, 2004.

Levenda, Peter. *Sinister Forces: A Grimoire of American Political Witchcraft. Book One: The Nine*. Oregon, USA, 2005.

Murray, Dr. Margaret Alice. *The God of the Witches*. USA, 2005.

Pinkham, Mark Amaru. *Guardians of the Holy Grail: The Knights Templar, John the Baptist, and the Water of Life*. Kempton, IL, USA, 2004

Simon. *Papal Magic: Occult Practices Within the Catholic Church*. New York, NY, USA, 2001.

Simpson, D.P. *Cassell's New Latin Dictionary*. New York, NY, USA, 1959.

Smith, Morton. *Jesus the Magician: Charlatan or Son of God*? USA,1998.

Summers, Montague. *Witchcraft and Black Magic*. USA, 2000.

Twyman, Tracy R. *Solomon's Treasure: The Magic and Mystery of America's Money*. Portland, OR, USA, 2005.